Nine-Patch
Blocks
&Quilts
for the ScrapSaver™

Judy Hopkins

Nine-Patch Blocks and Quilts for the ScrapSaver™
© 1992 by Judy Hopkins

That Patchwork Place, Inc., PO Box 118, Bothell, WA 98041-0118

Printed in the United States of America
97 96 95 94 93 92   6 5 4 3 2

Library of Congress Cataloging-in-Publication Data

Hopkins, Judy,
        Nine-patch blocks & quilts for the ScrapSaver / Judy Hopkins.
            p.   cm.
        ISBN 1-56477-001-X:
        1. Patchwork—Patterns.   2. Cutting
I. Title. II. Title: Nine-patch blocks & quilts for the ScrapSaver. III. Title: 9-patch blocks and quilts for the ScrapSaver.
TT835.H569 1992
746.46'041—dc20   91-44002
                                CIP

Credits

Photography by Doug Plager
Illustration and Graphics by
    Karin LaFramboise and
    Linda and Chris Gentry of Artworks
Cover Design by Judy Petry
Text Design by Choy-yee Kok
Editing by Barbara Weiland
Copy Editing by Liz McGehee

Acknowledgments

Special thanks are extended to:

    George Taylor, for his invaluable help in testing the ScrapSaver™ tool.
    Ella Bosse, Bonnie Bucknam, Jean Campbell, Jackie Carley, Debby Coates, Debbie Garrett, Alice Graves, Peggy Hinchey, Ruth Horvath, Mary McIver, Terri Shinn, Cathy Shultz, and Judy Wedemeyer for testing patterns and piecing blocks.

CONTENTS

GENERAL INFORMATION

Many members of the current generation of quiltmakers started quilting without the benefit of a scrap bag, a fabric source that was critical to the creation of many early quilts. Using modern tools and quick-cutting and -piecing techniques, quilters of the 1980s learned to capture the flavor of the scrap quilt by combining a large assortment of pieces cut from purchased or "collected" yardage. As we made more quilts, we began to accumulate scraps—but we found that our high-tech tools and efficient cutting methods were often useless in the face of an assortment of small, irregularly shaped pieces of fabric.

Faced with a daunting accumulation of scraps and limited time with which to deal with them, I started looking for ways to apply contemporary cutting methods to scrap fabrics. The result of my efforts was the ScrapSaver™, a tool for quick-cutting half-square triangles in an assortment of useful sizes from odd-shaped scraps.

Many blocks and quilts contain units made from half-square triangles. The twenty traditional blocks included in this book are made up of scrap half-square triangles and other simple shapes that can be quick-cut from scraps or yardage. The patterns include cutting and piecing instructions for the blocks, plans for quilts in several common sizes, and quilting suggestions. With this book and the ScrapSaver™, you can quickly transform your scraps into charming, classic quilts.

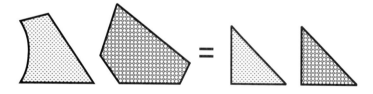

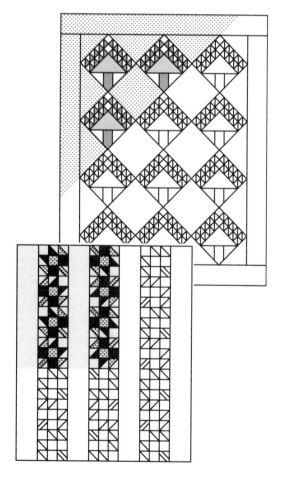

USING THE
SCRAPSAVER™ TOOL

To quick-cut half-square triangles, we typically add ⅞" to the desired finished size of a short side of the triangle, cut a square to that measurement, and divide the square on the diagonal. This technique allows for ¼" seams and yields two half-square triangles, with the short sides on the straight grain of the fabric and the long side on the bias.

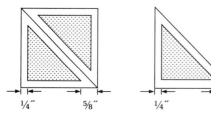

Finished size of short side
of triangle plus ⅞" = cut size

With the ScrapSaver™ tool, half-square triangles can be quick-cut individually, without first cutting a square. The tool is marked for cutting 1⅞", 2⅜", 2⅞", 3⅜", and 3⅞" half-square triangles; with ¼" seams, the short sides will finish to 1", 1½", 2", 2½", and 3".

To use the ScrapSaver™, you will need a rotary cutter and a cutting mat. A small cutting mat is very useful, as you can rotate the mat to get the proper cutting angle without disturbing the fabric. Press your scraps before you begin, then cut as described in the following paragraphs. Several scraps can be stacked for cutting. Place the largest piece on the bottom and the smallest piece on the top, aligning any square corners or true bias edges.

Remember:

For 1" (finished) triangles, use the 1⅞" lines.
For 1½" (finished) triangles, use the 2⅜" lines.
For 2" (finished) triangles, use the 2⅞" lines.
For 2½" (finished) triangles, use the 3⅜" lines.
For 3" (finished) triangles, use the 3⅞" lines.

For scraps with square corners:

Align the corner of the scrap with the proper edge-triangle lines of the ScrapSaver™ and cut along the straight edge to remove the excess fabric.

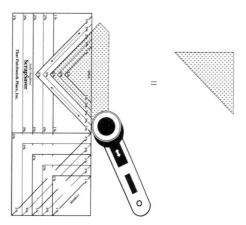

For scraps with true bias edges:

Align the bias edge of the scrap with the proper corner-triangle line of the ScrapSaver™ and cut along the two straight edges to remove the excess fabric.

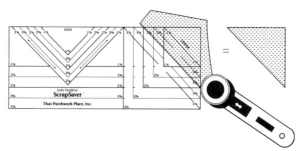

For scraps with no square corners or true bias edges:

Lay the corner triangle of the ScrapSaver™ over the scrap, aligning the ruler with the grain of the fabric and making sure that the corner-triangle line for the size you wish to cut does not extend beyond the fabric. Cut along the two straight edges, making a square corner.

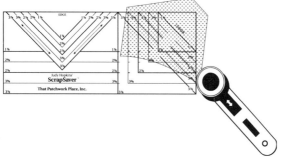

Align the square corner with the proper edge-triangle lines and cut along the straight edge to remove the excess fabric.

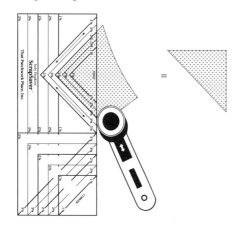

For larger scraps:

Lay the corner square of the ScrapSaver™ over the scrap, aligning the ruler with the grain of the fabric and making sure that the corner-square lines for the size you wish to cut do not extend beyond the fabric. Cut along the two straight edges, making a square corner.

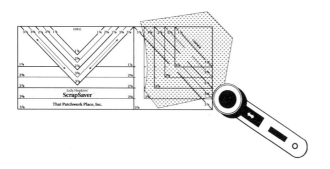

Rotate the cutting mat or turn the cut piece of fabric, align the corner you just cut with the proper corner-square lines, and cut along the two straight edges again to make a square.

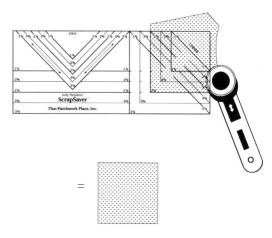

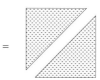

Align a corner of the square with the proper edge-triangle lines and cut along the straight edge to divide the square into two triangles.

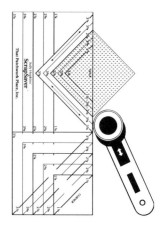

For large rectangular scraps:

Align a long edge of the ScrapSaver™ with the grain of the fabric and cut along the ruler to remove the uneven edge of the scrap.

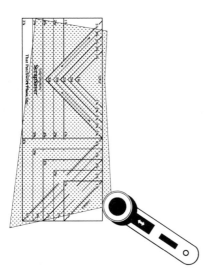

Rotate the cutting mat or turn the cut piece of fabric and align the proper long line with the straight cut you just made, letting the scrap extend just beyond the top of the ruler; cut along the two straight edges to make a square corner.

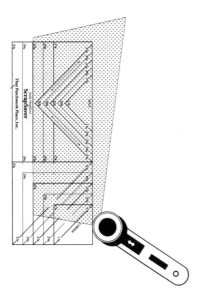

Align a square corner with the proper corner-square lines and cut along the straight edge to complete the square.

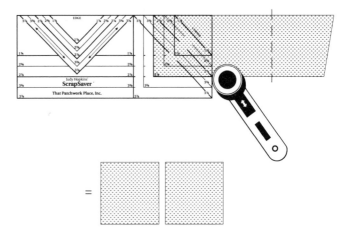

Repeat until you have cut as many squares as possible from the strip. Divide the squares, using the proper edge-triangle lines as shown on page 6.

USING THE PATTERNS FOR BLOCKS AND QUILTS

This book includes patterns for twenty traditional blocks that are made up of half-square triangles and other simple shapes. Half-square triangles up to 3" (finished) can be cut from scraps using the ScrapSaver™ tool. To quick-cut larger pieces, you will need a 6"- or 8"-square cutting guide marked in ⅛" increments. I recommend the Bias Square®. You may also need a 12"- or 15"-square cutting guide and a long cutting guide. Larger block pieces and setting pieces can be cut from scraps or from purchased or collected fabrics.

Two block outlines are given with each pattern. The first block outline is unshaded and includes letter designations for all pieces except the smallest triangles in the block. The second block outline is shaded to indicate value placement.

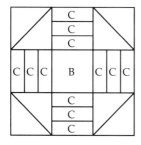 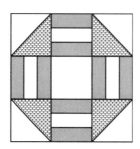

Some block patterns call for an assortment of light and dark fabrics, others for a combination of lights, mediums, and darks. Your fabric and color choices will depend on what is available in your scrap bag. The shaded outline may show only one or two "fabrics" for a particular value range; because you will be working with scraps, you may be using a number of different fabrics to represent a single value. When cutting the pieces shown as "dark" in the shaded outline, for example, you can use two, three, or ten different dark fabrics. These might be all the same color (like an assortment of dark blues) or different colors of the same value (like a combination of dark blues, dark greens, and browns).

It is difficult, and not really desirable, to maintain consistency in value and contrast in a scrap-bag quilt. Your "light" fabrics may range from light to medium, your "dark" fabrics from medium to dark. Contrast may vary from block to block; the pattern may stand out more in some areas of the quilt than in others. Remember, much of the charm of the scrap quilt lies in its unstudied variety. Simply do the best you can with what you have and enjoy the inconsistencies and contradictions that will invariably result.

The cutting instructions for most of the patterns given yield enough pieces to make a single block. For a few of the patterns, it is more efficient to cut the pieces for two blocks simultaneously; these are clearly marked. All cutting measurements include ¼" seam allowances; *do not add seam allowances to the dimensions given.*

Cutting directions for the smallest half-square triangles appear first, often followed by an instruction to join some or all of the triangles into half-square triangle units.

Next come cutting directions for the other block pieces, keyed to the lettered shapes in the unshaded block outline. You will need to use a different cutting guide to cut squares and rectangles; the ScrapSaver™ is not marked for cutting these shapes. When the block includes half-square triangles too large to be cut with the ScrapSaver™, you are instructed to cut a square and divide it on the diagonal. Use the Bias Square® to cut the square. Line up the cutting guide diagonally across the square, corner to corner, and cut.

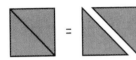

Most of the patterns in this book include instructions for quilts in five common sizes—crib, nap, twin, double, and queen. Fewer options are given when the block size or setting arrangement limits the available size range. The smallest-size quilt is illustrated with each pattern.

The quilt instructions spell out the block and setting piece requirements for each size quilt. Pertinent cutting dimensions for setting pieces are given with the individual quilt instructions; when the setting pieces are the same for all quilt sizes, those cutting dimensions appear below the block piecing diagrams. For quilts that are set on point, setting triangles are cut from squares. For corner triangles, cut two squares the given size and divide them once on the diagonal as shown above; for side triangles, cut squares the proper size and divide them *twice* on the diagonal, as shown:

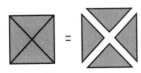

General instructions for finishing your quilt begin on page 30.

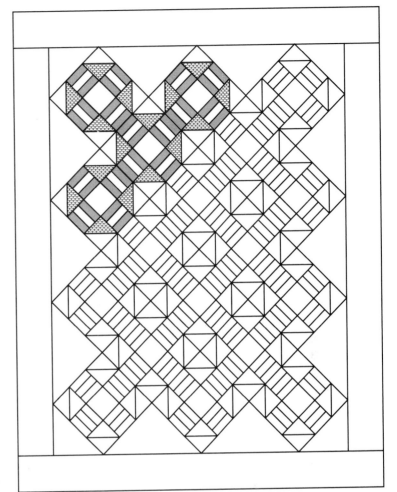

BASKET

12" block

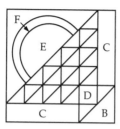 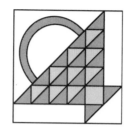

For *two* blocks:

Cut 18 ScrapSaver triangles, 2⅞", from medium fabrics.

Cut 32 ScrapSaver triangles, 2⅞", from dark fabrics.

Make 18 half-square triangle units.

Cut 1 square, 4⅞" x 4⅞", from light fabric; divide on the diagonal (B).

Cut 4 rectangles, 2½" x 8½", from light fabrics (C).

Cut 2 squares, 2½" x 2½", from medium fabrics (D).

Cut 1 square, 10⅞" x 10⅞", from light fabric; divide on the diagonal (E).

Using the template given on page 37, cut 2 handles from dark fabrics (F); appliqué to large triangles.

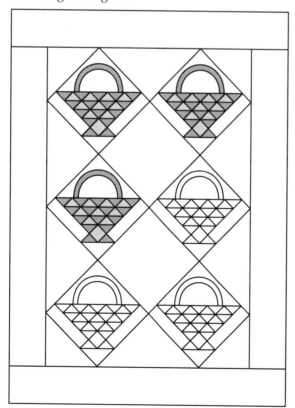

Piecing:

Appliqué handle to large triangle first

For the quilt shown in the drawing, you also will need:

Alternate blocks: Cut 12½" squares.

Corner triangles: Cut two 9⅜" squares; divide on the diagonal. ◻

Side triangles: Cut a 18¼" square for every 4 needed; divide *twice* on the diagonal. ⊠

See the quilt plans for the quilt size you are making to determine how many of these setting pieces to cut.

Quilt Plans:

Crib Quilt (42" x 59")
6 Basket blocks and 2 alternate blocks, set on point 2 across and 3 down; 4 corner triangles, 6 side triangles; 4" borders.

Nap Quilt (59" x 76")
12 Basket blocks and 6 alternate blocks, set on point 3 across and 4 down; 4 corner triangles, 10 side triangles; 4" borders.

Twin Bed Quilt (63" x 97")
15 Basket blocks and 8 alternate blocks, set on point 3 across and 5 down; 4 corner triangles, 12 side triangles; 6" borders.

Double Bed Quilt (80" x 97")
20 Basket blocks and 12 alternate blocks, set on point 4 across and 5 down; 4 corner triangles, 14 side triangles; 6" borders.

Queen Bed Quilt (84" x 101")
20 Basket blocks and 12 alternate blocks, set on point 4 across and 5 down; 4 corner triangles, 14 side triangles; 8" borders.

Quilting Suggestion:

Quilt alternate blocks with a floral design

Bear's Den

9" block

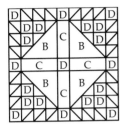 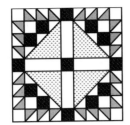

For one block:

Cut 36 ScrapSaver triangles, 1⅞", from light fabrics.

Cut 24 ScrapSaver triangles, 1⅞", from medium or dark fabrics.

    Make 24 half-square triangle units. ◪

Cut 4 ScrapSaver triangles, 3⅞", from light fabrics (B).

Cut 4 rectangles, 1½" x 3½", from light fabrics (C).

Cut 8 squares, 1½" x 1½", from light fabrics (D).

Cut 13 squares, 1½" x 1½", from medium or dark fabrics (D).

Piecing:

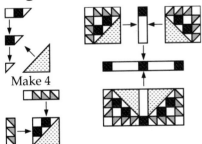

Make 4

For the quilt shown in the drawing, you also will need:

    Sashing pieces: Cut 2½" x 9½" rectangles.

    Sashing squares: Cut 2½" squares.

See the quilt plans for the quilt size you are making to determine how many of these setting pieces to cut.

Quilting Suggestion:

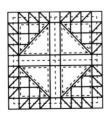

Quilt Plans:

Crib Quilt (43" x 54")
12 blocks, set 3 across and 4 down with 31 sashing pieces and 20 sashing squares; 4" borders.

Nap Quilt (58" x 69")
20 blocks, set 4 across and 5 down with 49 sashing pieces and 30 sashing squares; 6" borders.

Twin Bed Quilt (58" x 80")
24 blocks, set 4 across and 6 down with 58 sashing pieces and 35 sashing squares; 6" borders.

Double Bed Quilt (76" x 98")
48 blocks, set 6 across and 8 down with 110 sashing pieces and 63 sashing squares; 4" borders.

Queen Bed Quilt (80" x 102")
48 blocks, set 6 across and 8 down with 110 sashing pieces and 63 sashing squares; 6" borders.

CAT'S CRADLE

12" block

Block I   Block II

For one Block I:

Cut 6 ScrapSaver triangles, 2⅞", from light fabrics.

Cut 18 ScrapSaver triangles, 2⅞", from medium or dark fabrics.

    Make 6 half-square triangle units. ◩

Cut 3 squares, 4⅞" x 4⅞", from light fabrics; divide on the diagonal (B).

Cut 3 squares, 4½" x 4½", from light fabrics (C).

For one Block II:

Cut 6 ScrapSaver triangles, 2⅞", from medium or dark fabrics.

Cut 18 ScrapSaver triangles, 2⅞", from light fabrics.

    Make 6 half-square triangle units. ◩

Cut 3 squares, 4⅞" x 4⅞", from medium or dark fabrics; divide on the diagonal (B).

Cut 3 squares, 4½" x 4½", from medium or dark fabrics (C).

Piecing:

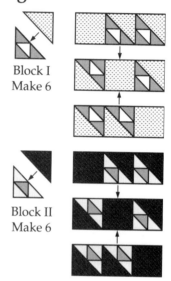

Block I
Make 6

Block II
Make 6

Quilt Plans:

Nap Quilt (52" x 76")
8 Block I and 7 Block II, set 3 across and 5 down; 8" borders.

Double Bed Quilt (72" x 96")
18 Block I and 17 Block II, set 5 across and 7 down; 6" borders.

Queen Bed Quilt (76" x 100")
18 Block I and 17 Block II, set 5 across and 7 down; 8" borders.

Quilting Suggestion:

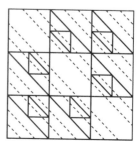

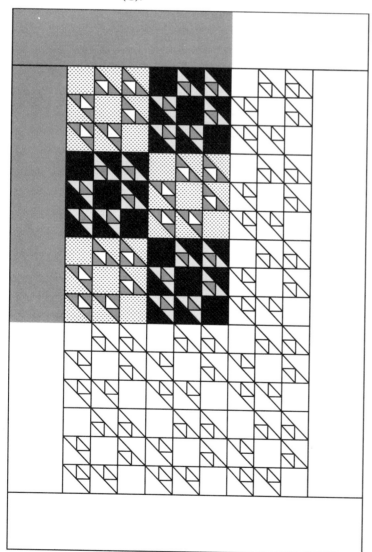

CONTRARY WIFE

7½" block

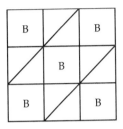 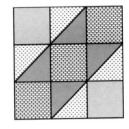

For one block:

Cut 4 ScrapSaver triangles, 3⅜", from light fabrics.

Cut 4 ScrapSaver triangles, 3⅜", from dark fabrics.

   Make 4 half-square triangle units.

Cut 5 squares, 3" x 3", from medium fabrics (B).

Piecing:

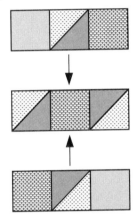

Quilting Suggestion:

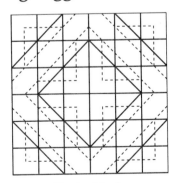

Center blocks

Quilt Plans:

Crib Quilt (42" x 57")
24 blocks, set 4 across and 6 down; 6" borders.

Nap Quilt (54" x 69")
48 blocks, set 6 across and 8 down; 4½" borders.

Twin Bed Quilt (57" x 87")
60 blocks, set 6 across and 10 down; 6" borders.

Double Bed Quilt (72" x 87")
80 blocks, set 8 across and 10 down; 6" borders.

Queen Bed Quilt (84" x 99")
120 blocks, set 10 across and 12 down; 4½" borders.

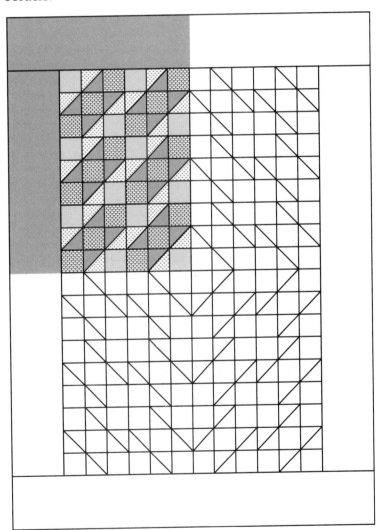

CUT GLASS DISH

12" block

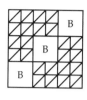

Block I   Block II

For one Block I:

Cut 24 ScrapSaver triangles, 2⅞", from light fabrics.

Cut 24 ScrapSaver triangles, 2⅞", from medium or dark fabrics.

Make 24 half-square triangle units.

Cut 3 squares, 4½" x 4½", from medium or dark fabrics. (B)

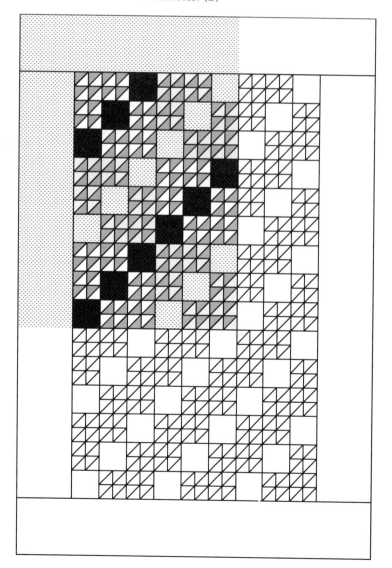

For one Block II:

Cut 24 ScrapSaver triangles, 2⅞", from light fabrics.

Cut 24 ScrapSaver triangles, 2⅞", from medium or dark fabrics.

Make 24 half-square triangle units.

Cut 3 squares, 4½" x 4½", from light fabrics (B).

Piecing:

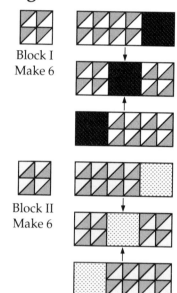

Block I
Make 6

Block II
Make 6

Quilt Plans:

Nap Quilt (52" x 76")
8 Block I and 7 Block II, set 3 across and 5 down; 8" borders.

Double Bed Quilt (72" x 96")
18 Block I and 17 Block II, set 5 across and 7 down; 6" borders.

Queen Bed Quilt (76" x 100")
18 Block I and 17 Block II, set 5 across and 7 down; 8" borders.

Quilting Suggestion:

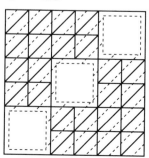

DARTING BIRD

9" block

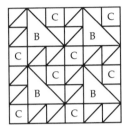 

For one block:

Cut 24 ScrapSaver triangles, 2⅜", from light fabrics.
Cut 8 ScrapSaver triangles, 2⅜", from medium fabrics.
Cut 8 ScrapSaver triangles, 2⅜", from dark fabrics.
    Make 8 light/medium and 8 light/dark half-square triangle units.
Cut 2 ScrapSaver triangles, 3⅞", from medium fabrics (B).
Cut 2 ScrapSaver triangles, 3⅞", from dark fabrics (B).
Cut 4 squares, 2" x 2", from light fabrics (C).
Cut 2 squares, 2" x 2", from medium fabrics (C).
Cut 2 squares, 2" x 2", from dark fabrics (C).

Piecing:

Make 2 dark birds

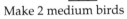
Make 2 medium birds

For the quilt shown in the drawing, you also will need:
    Alternate blocks: Cut 9½" squares.
See the quilt plans for the quilt size you are making to determine how many of these setting pieces to cut.

Quilting Suggestion:

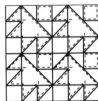
Quilt alternate blocks with clouds or sunbeams

Quilt Plans:

Crib Quilt (39" x 57")
8 Darting Bird blocks and 7 alternate blocks, set 3 across and 5 down; 6" borders.
Nap Quilt (54" x 72")
18 Darting Bird blocks and 17 alternate blocks, set 5 across and 7 down; 4½" borders.
Twin Bed Quilt (57" x 93")
23 Darting Bird blocks and 22 alternate blocks, set 5 across and 9 down; 6" borders.
Double Bed Quilt (72" x 90")
32 Darting Bird blocks and 31 alternate blocks, set 7 across and 9 down; 4½" borders.
Queen Bed Quilt (81" x 99")
32 Darting Bird blocks and 31 alternate blocks, set 7 across and 9 down; 9" borders.

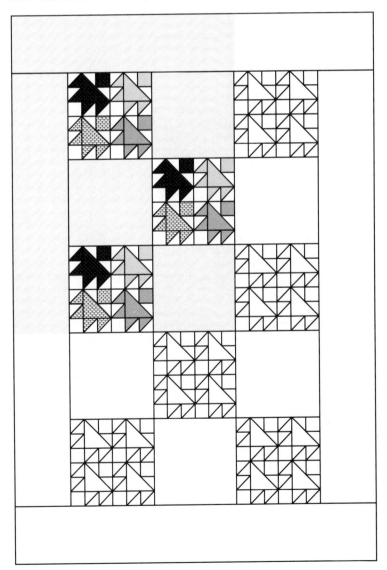

DOUBLE SAWTOOTH

12" block

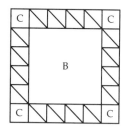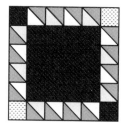

Piecing:

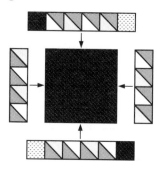

For one block:

Cut 16 ScrapSaver triangles, 2⅞", from light fabrics.

Cut 16 ScrapSaver triangles, 2⅞", from medium or dark fabrics.

    Make 16 half-square triangle units. ◣

Cut 1 square, 8½" x 8½", from medium or dark fabric (B).

Cut 2 squares, 2½" x 2½", from light fabrics (C).

Cut 2 squares, 2½" x 2½", from medium or dark fabrics (C).

Quilt Plans:

Crib Quilt (48" x 60")
12 blocks, set 3 across and 4 down; 6" borders.
Nap Quilt (60" x 72")
20 blocks, set 4 across and 5 down; 6" borders.
Twin Bed Quilt (60" x 84")
24 blocks, set 4 across and 6 down; 6" borders.
Double Bed Quilt (72" x 96")
35 blocks, set 5 across and 7 down; 6" borders.
Queen Bed Quilt (84" x 96")
42 blocks, set 6 across and 7 down; 6" borders.

Quilting Suggestion:

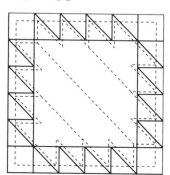

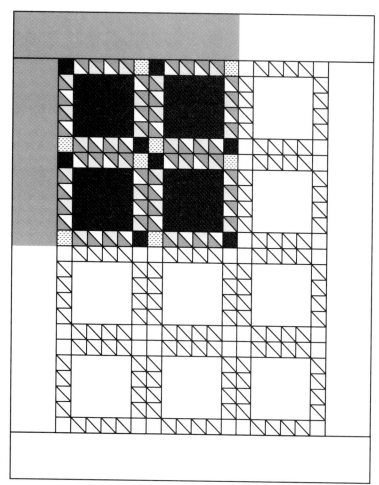

DOUBLE X

12" block

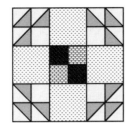

For one block:

Cut 12 ScrapSaver triangles, 2⅞", from light fabrics.

Cut 12 ScrapSaver triangles, 2⅞", from medium or dark fabrics.

Make 12 half-square triangle units. ◩

Cut 4 squares, 4½" x 4½", from light fabrics (B).

Cut 4 squares, 2½" x 2½", from light fabrics (C).

Cut 4 squares, 2½" x 2½", from medium or dark fabrics (C).

Piecing:

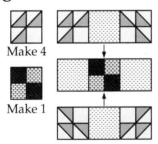

Make 4

Make 1

For the quilt shown in the drawing, you also will need:

Alternate blocks: Cut 12½" squares.

See the quilt plans for the quilt size you are making to determine how many of these setting pieces to cut.

Quilting Suggestion:

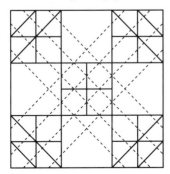

Use the same quilting pattern in alternate blocks

Quilt Plans:

Nap Quilt (52" x 76")
8 Double X blocks and 7 alternate blocks, set 3 across and 5 down; 8" borders.

Double Bed Quilt (72" x 96")
18 Double X blocks and 17 alternate blocks, set 5 across and 7 down; 6" borders.

Queen Bed Quilt (76" x 100")
18 Double X blocks and 17 alternate blocks, set 5 across and 7 down; 8" borders.

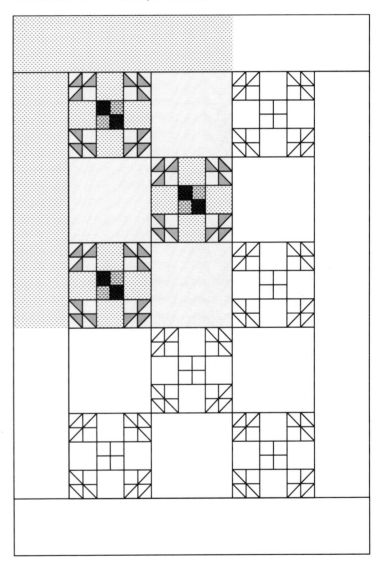

GARDEN PATH

15" block

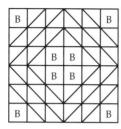
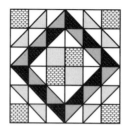

For one block:

Cut 28 ScrapSaver triangles, 3⅜", from light fabrics.

Cut 8 ScrapSaver triangles, 3⅜", from medium fabrics.

Cut 20 ScrapSaver triangles, 3⅜", from dark fabrics.

Make 8 light/medium and 20 light/dark half-square triangle units. ◪

Cut 8 squares, 3" x 3", from medium fabrics (B).

Piecing:

Make 4

Quilt Plans:

Crib Quilt (42" x 57")
6 blocks, set 2 across and 3 down; 6" borders.

Nap Quilt (57" x 72")
12 blocks, set 3 across and 4 down; 6" borders.

Twin Bed Quilt (57" x 87")
15 blocks, set 3 across and 5 down; 6" borders.

Double Bed Quilt (75" x 90")
20 blocks, set 4 across and 5 down; 7½" borders.

Queen Bed Quilt (84" x 99")
30 blocks, set 5 across and 6 down; 4½" borders.

Quilting Suggestion:

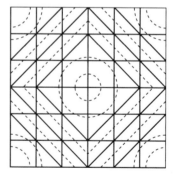

GOLDEN GATE

9" block

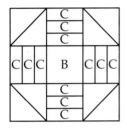 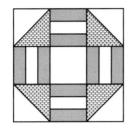

For one block:

Cut 4 ScrapSaver triangles, 3⅞", from light fabrics.

Cut 4 ScrapSaver triangles, 3⅞", from medium fabrics.

Make 4 half-square triangle units. ◢

Cut 1 square, 3½" x 3½", from light fabric (B).

Cut 4 rectangles, 1½" x 3½", from light fabrics (C)

Cut 8 rectangles, 1½" x 3½", from dark fabrics (C).

Piecing:

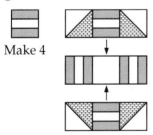

Make 4

For the quilt shown in the drawing, you also will need:

Corner triangles: Cut two 7¼" squares; divide on the diagonal. ◻

Side triangles: Cut a 14" square for every 4 needed; divide *twice* on the diagonal. ⊠

See the quilt plans for the quilt size you are making to determine how many of these setting pieces to cut.

Quilting Suggestion:

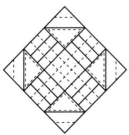

Quilt Plan:

Crib Quilt (47" x 60")
18 blocks, set on point 3 across and 4 down; 4 corner triangles, 10 side triangles; 4½" borders.

Nap Quilt (60" x 72½")
32 blocks, set on point 4 across and 5 down; 4 corner triangles, 14 side triangles; 4½" borders.

Twin Bed Quilt (60" x 85½")
39 blocks, set on point 4 across and 6 down; 4 corner triangles, 16 side triangles; 4½" borders.

Double Bed Quilt (72½" x 85½")
50 blocks, set on point 5 across and 6 down; 4 corner triangles, 18 side triangles; 4½" borders.

Queen Bed Quilt (85½" x 98")
72 blocks, set on point 6 across and 7 down; 4 corner triangles, 22 side triangles; 4½" borders.

Maple Leaf

7½" block

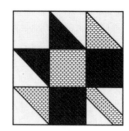 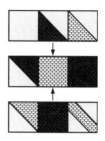

For one block:

Cut 4 ScrapSaver triangles, 3⅜", from light fabrics.

Cut 4 ScrapSaver triangles, 3⅜", from medium or dark fabrics.

Make 4 half-square triangle units. ◢

Cut 2 squares, 3" x 3", from light fabrics (B).

Cut 3 squares, 3" x 3", from medium or dark fabrics (B).

Using the template given on page 37, cut 1 stem from medium or dark fabric (C); appliqué to one of the light squares.

Piecing:

Appliqué stem to light square first

Quilt Plans:

Crib Quilt (42½" x 52½")
21 blocks, set in 3 seven-block strips; 4 vertical bars made from 5½" x 53" strips.

Nap Quilt (55" x 75")
40 blocks, set in 4 ten-block strips; 5 vertical bars made from 5½" x 75½" strips.

Twin Bed Quilt (67½" x 90")
60 blocks, set in 5 twelve-block strips; 6 vertical bars made from 5½" x 90½" strips.

Double Bed Quilt (73" x 90")
72 blocks, set in 6 twelve-block strips; 7 vertical bars made from 4½" x 90½" strips.

Queen Bed Quilt (80" x 97½")
78 blocks, set in 6 thirteen-block strips; 7 vertical bars made from 5½" x 98" strips.

Quilting Suggestion:

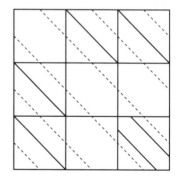

Quilt bars with diagonal lines running the opposite direction

NINE-PATCH STAR

9" block

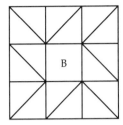
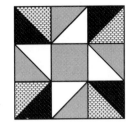

For one block:

Cut 4 ScrapSaver triangles, 3⅞", from light fabrics.

Cut 4 ScrapSaver triangles, 3⅞", from medium fabrics.

Cut 8 ScrapSaver triangles, 3⅞", from dark fabrics.

Make 4 light/dark and 4 medium/dark half-square triangle units.

Cut 1 square, 3½" x 3½", from dark fabric (B).

Piecing:

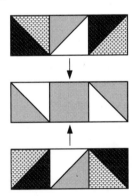

Quilting Suggestion:

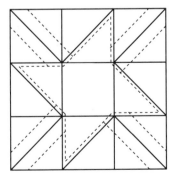

Quilt Plans:

Crib Quilt (45" x 54")
20 blocks, set 4 across and 5 down; 4½" borders.

Nap Quilt (54" x 72")
35 blocks, set 5 across and 7 down; 4½" borders.

Twin Bed Quilt (57" x 84")
40 blocks, set 5 across and 8 down; 6" borders.

Double Bed Quilt (75" x 93")
63 blocks, set 7 across and 9 down; 6" borders.

Queen Bed Quilt (84" x 102")
80 blocks, set 8 across and 10 down; 6" borders.

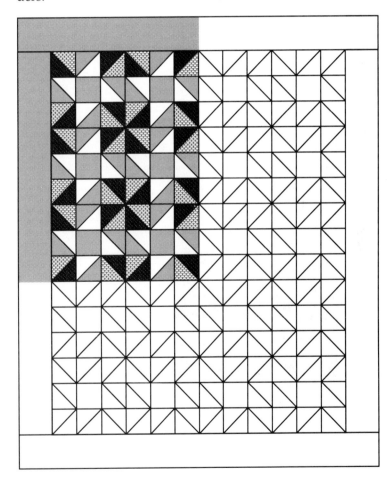

PRAIRIE QUEEN

9" block

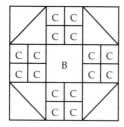 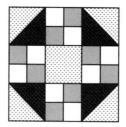

For one block:

Cut 4 ScrapSaver triangles, 3⅞", from light fabrics.

Cut 4 ScrapSaver triangles, 3⅞", from medium or dark fabrics.

   Make 4 half-square triangle units. ◪

Cut 1 square, 3½" x 3½", from light fabric (B).

Cut 8 squares, 2" x 2", from light fabrics (C).

Cut 8 squares, 2" x 2", from medium or dark fabrics (C).

Piecing:

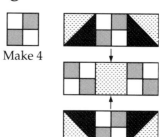

Make 4

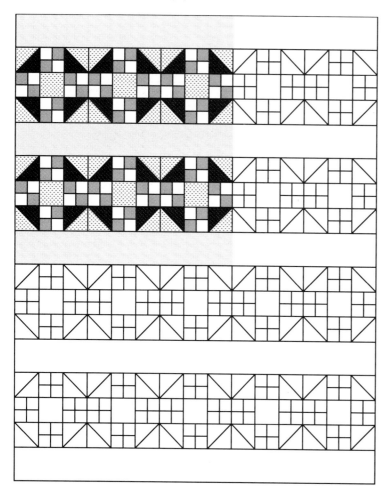

Quilt Plans:

Crib Quilt (45" x 58½")
20 blocks, set in 4 five-block rows; 5 horizontal bars made from 5" x 45½" strips.

Nap Quilt (54" x 72")
30 blocks, set in 5 six-block rows; 6 horizontal bars made from 5" x 54½" strips.

Twin Bed Quilt (63" x 85½")
42 blocks, set in 6 seven-block rows; 7 horizontal bars made from 5" x 63½" strips.

Double Bed Quilt (72" x 99")
56 blocks, set in 7 eight-block rows; 8 horizontal bars made from 5" x 72½" strips.

Queen Bed Quilt (81" x 99")
63 blocks, set in 7 nine-block rows; 8 horizontal bars made from 5" x 81½" strips.

Quilting Suggestion:

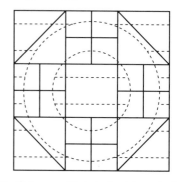

Quilt bars with interlocking circles

PREMIUM STAR

13½" block

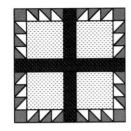

For one block:

Cut 24 ScrapSaver triangles, 2⅜", from light fabrics.
Cut 24 ScrapSaver triangles, 2⅜", from medium or dark fabrics.
  Make 24 half-square triangle units.
Cut 4 squares, 5" x 5", from light fabrics (B).
Cut 4 squares, 2" x 2", from medium or dark fabrics (C).
Cut 2 rectangles, 2" x 6½", from medium or dark fabrics (D).
Cut 1 rectangle, 2" x 14", from medium or dark fabric (E).

Piecing:

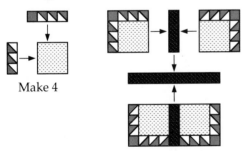

Make 4

For the quilt shown in the drawing, you also will need:
  Sashing pieces: Cut 3½" x 14" rectangles. See the quilt plans for the quilt size you are making to determine how many of these setting pieces to cut. Cutting dimensions for the sashing strips are given with the individual quilt plans.

Quilting Suggestion:

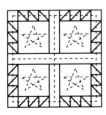

Quilt Plans:

Crib Quilt (42" x 58½")
6 blocks, set 2 across and 3 down with 3 sashing pieces and 2 sashing strips, 3½" x 42½"; 6" borders.

Nap Quilt (58½" x 75")
12 blocks, set 3 across and 4 down with 8 sashing pieces and 3 sashing strips, 3½" x 59"; 6" borders.

Twin Bed Quilt (58½" x 91½")
15 blocks, set 3 across and 5 down with 10 sashing pieces and 4 sashing strips, 3½" x 59"; 6" borders.

Double Bed Quilt (75" x 91½")
20 blocks, set 4 across and 5 down with 15 sashing pieces and 4 sashing strips, 3½" x 75½"; 6" borders.

Queen Bed Quilt (81" x 97½")
20 blocks, set 4 across and 5 down with 15 sashing pieces and 4 sashing strips, 3½" x 81½"; 9" borders.

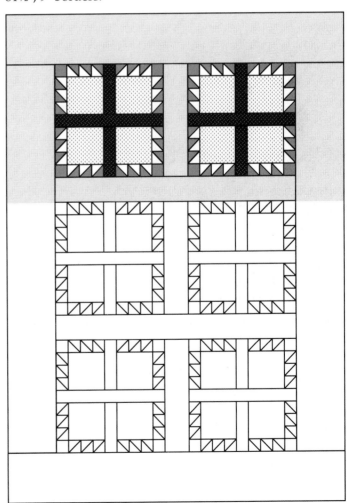

ROBBING PETER TO PAY PAUL

12" block

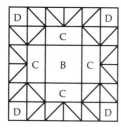 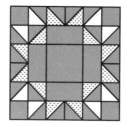

For one block:

Cut 20 ScrapSaver triangles, 2⅞", from light fabrics.

Cut 20 ScrapSaver triangles, 2⅞", from medium or dark fabrics.

Make 20 half-square triangle units. ◪

Cut 1 square, 4½" x 4½", from medium or dark fabric (B).

Cut 4 rectangles, 2½" x 4½", from medium or dark fabrics (C).

Cut 4 squares, 2½" x 2½", from medium or dark fabrics (D).

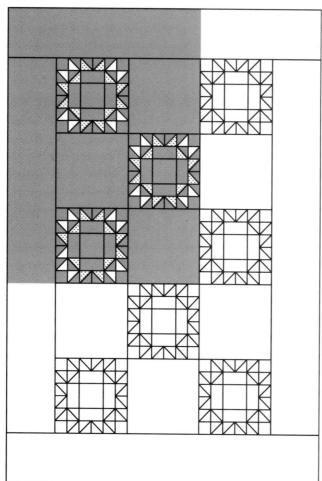

Piecing:

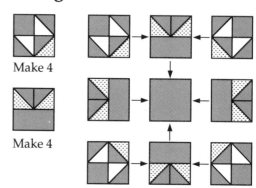

Make 4

Make 4

For the quilt shown in the drawing, you also will need:

Alternate blocks: Cut 12½" squares.

See the quilt plans for the quilt size you are making to determine how many of these setting pieces to cut.

Quilt Plans:

Nap Quilt (52" x 76")
8 Robbing Peter to Pay Paul blocks and 7 alternate blocks, set 3 across and 5 down; 8" borders.

Double Bed Quilt (72" x 96")
18 Robbing Peter to Pay Paul blocks and 17 alternate blocks, set 5 across and 7 down; 6" borders.

Queen Bed Quilt (76" x 100")
18 Robbing Peter to Pay Paul blocks and 17 alternate blocks, set 5 across and 7 down; 8" borders.

Quilting Suggestion:

Use the same quilting pattern
in alternate blocks

ROCKY ROAD TO CALIFORNIA

9" block

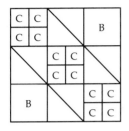 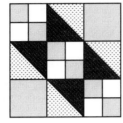

For one block:

Cut 4 ScrapSaver triangles, 3⅞", from light fabrics.

Cut 4 ScrapSaver triangles, 3⅞", from dark fabrics.

Make 4 half-square triangle units. ◣

Cut 2 squares, 3½" x 3½", from medium fabrics (B).

Cut 6 squares, 2" x 2", from light fabrics (C).

Cut 6 squares, 2" x 2", from medium fabrics (C).

Piecing:

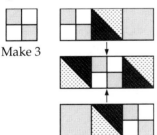

Make 3

Quilting Suggestion:

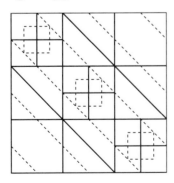

Quilt Plans:

Crib Quilt (45" x 63")
24 blocks, set 4 across and 6 down; 4½" borders.

Nap Quilt (54" x 72")
24 blocks, set 4 across and 6 down; 9" borders.

Twin Bed Quilt (63" x 81")
48 blocks, set 6 across and 8 down; 4½" borders.

Double Bed Quilt (72" x 90")
48 blocks, set 6 across and 8 down; 9" borders.

Queen Bed Quilt (84" x 102")
80 blocks, set 8 across and 10 down; 6" borders.

ROSEBUD

9" block

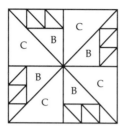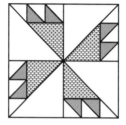

For one block:

Cut 12 ScrapSaver triangles, 2⅜", from light fabrics.

Cut 8 ScrapSaver triangles, 2⅜", from dark fabrics.

Make 8 half-square triangle units. ◣

Cut 4 ScrapSaver triangles, 3⅞", from medium fabrics (B).

Cut 2 squares, 5⅜" x 5⅜", from light fabrics; divide on the diagonal (C).

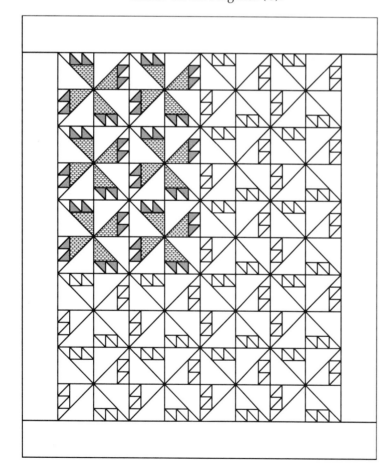

Piecing:

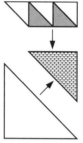

Make 4

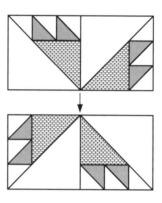

Quilt Plans:

Crib Quilt (45" x 54")
20 blocks, set 4 across and 5 down; 4½" borders.

Nap Quilt (54" x 72")
35 blocks, set 5 across and 7 down; 4½" borders.

Twin Bed Quilt (57" x 84")
40 blocks, set 5 across and 8 down; 6" borders.

Double Bed Quilt (75" x 93")
63 blocks, set 7 across and 9 down; 6" borders.

Queen Bed Quilt (84" x 102")
80 blocks, set 8 across and 10 down; 6" borders.

Quilting Suggestion:

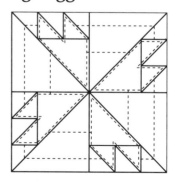

SHOOFLY

3" block

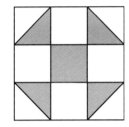

For one block:

Cut 4 ScrapSaver triangles, 1⅞", from light fabrics.
Cut 4 ScrapSaver triangles, 1⅞", from medium or dark fabrics.
   Make 4 half-square triangle units. ◪
Cut 4 squares, 1½" x 1½", from light fabrics (B).
Cut 1 square, 1½" x 1½", from medium or dark fabric (B).
Cut 4 squares, 3½" x 3½", from light fabrics for small alternate blocks (C) to make nine-patch groups.

Piecing:

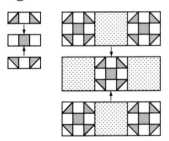

Join into nine-patch groups

For the quilt shown in the drawing, you also will need:
   Large alternate blocks: Cut 9½" squares. See the quilt plans for the quilt size you are making to determine how many of these setting pieces to cut.

Quilting Suggestion:

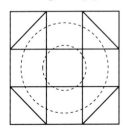

Quilt alternate blocks with more concentric circles

Quilt Plans:

Crib Quilt (39" x 57")
8 Shoofly groups and 7 large alternate blocks, set 3 across and 5 down; 6" borders.
Nap Quilt (54" x 72")
18 Shoofly groups and 17 large alternate blocks, set 5 across and 7 down; 4½" borders.
Twin Bed Quilt (57" x 93")
23 Shoofly groups and 22 large alternate blocks, set 5 across and 9 down; 6" borders.
Double Bed Quilt (72" x 90")
32 Shoofly groups and 31 large alternate blocks, set 7 across and 9 down; 4½" borders.
Queen Bed Quilt (81" x 99")
32 Shoofly groups and 31 large alternate blocks, set 7 across and 9 down; 9" borders.

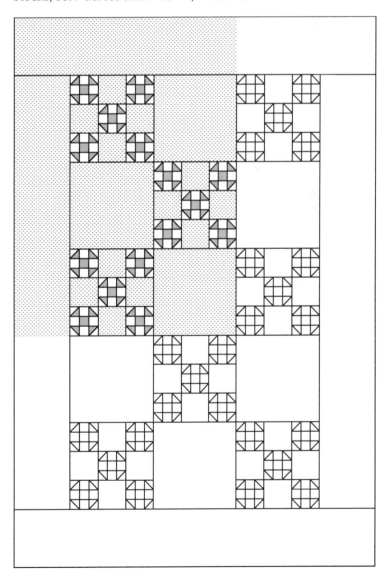

TEMPERANCE TREE

9" block

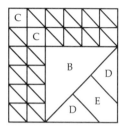 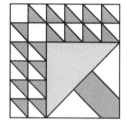

For *two* blocks:

Cut 36 ScrapSaver triangles, 2⅜", from light fabrics.

Cut 36 ScrapSaver triangles, 2⅜", from dark fabrics.

   Make 36 half-square triangle units.

Cut 1 square, 6⅞" x 6⅞", from medium fabric; divide on the diagonal (B).

Cut 4 squares, 2" x 2", from light fabrics (C).

Cut 1 square, 5¾" x 5¾", from light fabric; divide *twice* on the diagonal (D).

Using the template given on page 37, cut 2 tree trunks from dark fabrics (E).

Piecing:

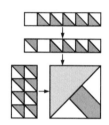

For the quilt shown in the drawing, you also will need:

   Alternate blocks: Cut 9½" squares.

   Corner triangles: Cut two 7¼" squares; divide on the diagonal. ◻

   Side triangles: Cut a 14" square for every 4 needed; divide *twice* on the diagonal. ⊠

See the quilt plans for the quilt size you are making to determine how many of these setting pieces to cut.

Quilt Plans:

Crib Quilt (47" x 60")
12 tree blocks and 6 alternate blocks, set on point 3 across and 4 down; 4 corner triangles, 10 side triangles; 4½" borders.

Nap Quilt (60" x 72½")
20 tree blocks and 12 alternate blocks, set on point 4 across and 5 down; 4 corner triangles, 14 side triangles; 4½" borders.

Twin Bed Quilt (60" x 85½")
24 tree blocks and 15 alternate blocks, set on point 4 across and 6 down; 4 corner triangles, 16 side triangles; 4½" borders.

Double Bed Quilt (72½" x 85½")
30 tree blocks and 20 alternate blocks, set on point 5 across and 6 down; 4 corner triangles, 18 side triangles; 4½" borders.

Queen Bed Quilt (85½" x 98")
42 tree blocks and 30 alternate blocks, set on point 6 across and 7 down; 4 corner triangles, 22 side triangles; 4½" borders.

Quilting Suggestion:

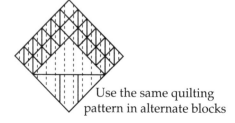

Use the same quilting pattern in alternate blocks

TIARA

6" block

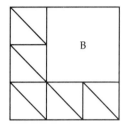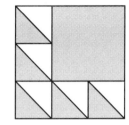

For one block:

Cut 5 ScrapSaver triangles, 2⅞", from light fabrics.
Cut 5 ScrapSaver triangles, 2⅞", from medium or dark fabrics.
   Make 5 half-square triangle units. ◣
Cut 1 square, 4½" x 4½", from medium or dark fabric (B).

Piecing:

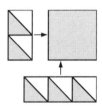

For the quilt shown in the drawing, you also will need:
   Alternate blocks: Cut 6½" squares.
   Corner triangles: Cut two 5⅛" squares; divide on the diagonal. ◻
   Side triangles: Cut a 9¾" square for every 4 needed; divide *twice* on the diagonal. ◻
See the quilt plans for the quilt size you are making to determine how many of these setting pieces to cut.

Quilting Suggestion:

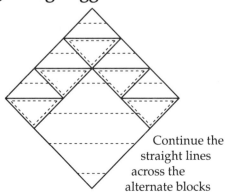

Continue the straight lines across the alternate blocks

Quilt Plans:

Crib Quilt (46" x 54½")
20 Tiara blocks and 12 alternate blocks, set on point 4 across and 5 down; 4 corner triangles, 14 side triangles; 6" borders.
Nap Quilt (54½" x 71½")
35 Tiara blocks and 24 alternate blocks, set on point 5 across and 7 down; 4 corner triangles, 20 side triangles; 6" borders.
Twin Bed Quilt (59" x 84½")
54 Tiara blocks and 40 alternate blocks, set on point 6 across and 9 down; 4 corner triangles, 26 side triangles; 4" borders.
Double Bed Quilt (71½" x 88½")
63 Tiara blocks and 48 alternate blocks, set on point 7 across and 9 down; 4 corner triangles, 28 side triangles; 6" borders.
Queen Bed Quilt (84½" x 101½")
99 Tiara blocks and 80 alternate blocks, set on point 9 across and 11 down; 4 corner triangles, 36 side triangles; 4" borders.

FINISHING YOUR QUILT

Squaring Up Blocks

Some quiltmakers find it necessary to trim or square up their blocks before they assemble them into a quilt top. If you trim, be sure to leave ¼" seam allowance beyond any points or other important block details that fall at the outside edges of the block.

To square up blocks, cut a piece of plastic-coated freezer paper to the proper size (finished block size plus seam allowance); iron the freezer paper to your ironing board cover, plastic side down. Pin the block edges to the edges of the freezer-paper guide and gently steam press; let the blocks cool before you unpin them.

Straight Sets

In straight sets, blocks are laid out in rows that parallel the edges of the quilt. Constructing a straight-set quilt is simple and straightforward. When blocks are to be set side by side without sashing, simply stitch them together in rows; then, join the rows to complete the patterned section of the quilt. If alternate blocks are called for, lay out the primary and alternate blocks in checkerboard fashion and stitch the rows. Cutting dimensions are given when a pattern calls for alternate blocks.

When setting blocks together with plain sashing, join the sashing pieces and the blocks to form rows, starting and ending each row with a block. Then, join the rows with the long sashing strips. Make sure that the corners of the blocks are aligned when you stitch the rows together. Cutting dimensions are given when a pattern calls for sashing.

If your sashing includes corner squares of a different color or fabric than the rest of the sashing (sashing squares), join the vertical sashing pieces to the blocks to form rows, starting and ending each

row with a sashing piece. Join the sashing squares to the horizontal sashing pieces to make sashing strips, starting and ending each row with a sashing square. Join the rows of blocks with these long, pieced sashing strips. Cutting dimensions are given when a pattern calls for sashing with sashing squares.

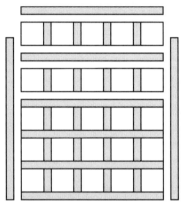
Plain sashing with sashing strips

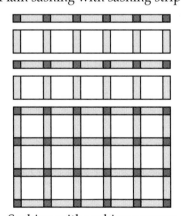
Sashing with sashing squares

On-Point Sets

Quilts laid out with the blocks set on point are constructed in diagonal rows, with half- and quarter-square setting triangles added to complete the corners and sides of the quilt. Cutting dimensions are given when a pattern calls for setting triangles. Lay out all the blocks and setting pieces in the proper configuration before you start sewing. Pick up and sew one diagonal row at a time; then, join the rows. Trim edges and square up corners, if necessary, before adding borders; be sure to leave ¼" seam allowances around the outside edges of the quilt.

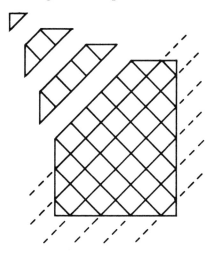

Assembly Diagram for On-Point Set

Some of us have difficulty getting on-point quilts to lie flat. You can minimize potential problems by taking a few precautions during the cutting and assembly process. Make sure that the individual blocks are absolutely square and are all the same size. Alternate blocks should be perfectly square and exactly the same size as the primary blocks. The 90° corners of the side setting triangles should be truly square. Since these triangles are quick-cut on the bias, sometimes the corners are not square; it's worth taking the time to double-check. When you join blocks to setting triangles, feed them into the sewing machine with the block, which has a straight-grain edge, on top and the bias-edged setting triangle on the bottom.

Borders

Because extra yardage is required to cut borders on the lengthwise grain, plain border strips commonly are cut along the crosswise grain and seamed when extra length is needed. These seams should be pressed open for minimum visibility. To ensure a flat, square quilt, cut border strips long and trim the strips to the proper size

after the actual dimensions of the patterned center section of the quilt are known.

To make a border with straight-cut corners, measure the length of the patterned section of the quilt at the center, from raw edge to raw edge. Cut two border strips to that measurement and join them to the sides of the quilt with a ¼" seam, matching the ends and centers and easing the edges to fit. Then, measure the width of the quilt at the center from edge to edge, including the border pieces that you just attached. Cut two border strips to that measurement and join them to the top and bottom of the quilt, matching ends and centers and easing as necessary.

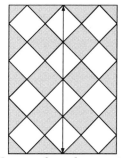 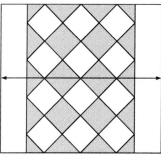

Measure length at *center*; cut and add side borders.

Measure width at center including side borders; cut and add top and bottom borders.

To make mitered corners, first estimate the finished outside dimensions of your quilt *including borders*. Border strips should be cut to this length plus 2"–3". If your quilt is to have multiple borders, sew the individual strips together and treat the resulting unit as a single piece for mitering.

Mark the centers of the quilt edges and the centers of the border strips. Stitch the borders to the quilt with a ¼" seam, matching the centers; the border strip should extend the same distance at each end of the quilt. Start and stop stitching ¼" from the corners of the quilt; press the seams toward the borders.

Lay the first corner to be mitered on the ironing board, pinning as necessary to keep the quilt from pulling and the corner from slipping. Fold one of the border units under, at a 45° angle. Work with the fold until seams or stripes meet properly; pin at the fold, then check to see that the outside corner is square and that there is no extra fullness at the edges. When everything is straight and square, press the fold.

Starting at the outside edge of the quilt, center a piece of 1" masking tape over the mitered fold; remove pins as you apply the tape.

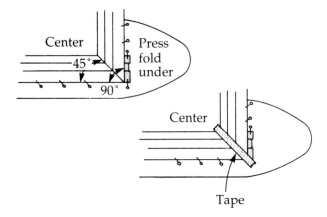

Unpin the quilt from the ironing board and turn it over. Fold the center section of the quilt diagonally from the corner, right sides together, and align the long edges of the border strips. Draw a light pencil line on the crease created when you pressed the fold. Stitch on the pencil line, then remove the tape; trim the excess fabric and press the seam open. Repeat these steps for the remaining three corners.

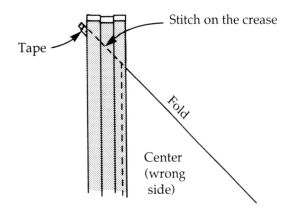

Marking the Quilting Lines

Premarking a quilting design will not be necessary if you are planning to quilt "in the ditch" or to outline quilt a uniform distance from seam lines. Some quiltmakers do outline quilting "by eye," though many others use ¼" masking tape to mark these lines as they stitch. You can use masking or drafting tape to mark any straight-line quilting design; simple shapes can be cut from Con-Tact® paper. Apply the tape or adhesive-paper shape when you are ready to quilt and remove promptly after you have quilted along its edge; adhesives left on the quilt may leave a residue that is difficult to remove.

More complex quilting designs should be marked on the quilt top before the quilt is layered with batting and backing. A gridded transparent ruler is useful for measuring and marking straight lines and filler grids. Quilting patterns from books or magazines or hand-drawn designs can be placed underneath the quilt and traced onto the fabric if the quilt fabrics are fairly light; use a light box or put your work against a window if you have difficulty seeing the design.

If you cannot see through the quilt fabric, the design will have to be drawn directly onto the quilt top. Use a precut plastic stencil, or make your own by drawing or tracing the quilting design on clear plastic; cut out the lines with a double-bladed craft knife, leaving "bridges" every inch or two so the stencil will hold its shape. Or, trace the design onto plain paper; cover the paper with one or two layers of clear Con-Tact® paper and cut out the lines. You can put small pieces of double-stick tape on the back of the stencil to keep it in place as you mark the quilting lines.

When marking quilting lines, work on a hard, smooth surface. Use a hard lead pencil (#3 or #4) on light fabrics; for dark fabrics, try a fine-line chalk marker or a silver, nonphoto blue or white pencil. Ideally, marking lines will remain visible for the duration of the quilting process and can be removed easily when the quilting is done. Light lines are always easier to remove than heavy ones; test to make sure that the markings will wash out after the quilting is completed.

Backings and Batting

The quilt backing should be at least 4" wider and longer than the quilt top. A length of 44"-wide fabric will be adequate to back a quilt that is no wider than 40". For a larger quilt, buy extra-wide cotton or sew two or more pieces of fabric together. Use a single fabric, seamed as necessary to make a backing of adequate size, or piece a simple multi-fabric back that complements the front of the quilt. Do not use bed sheets; the fabric is closely woven and difficult to quilt through.

If you opt for a seamed or pieced backing, trim off selvages before you stitch and press seams open. Seam single-fabric backings horizontally to conserve fabric.

Batting comes packaged in standard bed sizes; it also can be bought by the yard. Several weights, or thicknesses, are available. Thick battings are fine for tied quilts and comforters; choose a thinner batting if you intend to quilt by hand or machine.

Thin batting is available in 100% cotton, 100% polyester, and an 80%-20% cotton-polyester blend. This blend is said to combine the best features of the two fibers. All-cotton batting is soft and drapeable, but requires close quilting and produces quilts that are rather flat. Though many quilters like the antique look, some find cotton batting difficult to "needle." Glazed or bonded polyester batting is sturdy, easy to work with, and washes well. It requires less quilting than cotton and has more loft. However, polyester fibers sometimes migrate through fabric, creating tiny white "beards" on the surface of a quilt. The dark gray polyester battings now available are expected to ease this problem for quiltmakers who like to work with dark fabrics; bearding, if it occurs, will be less noticeable.

Unroll your batting and let it relax overnight before you layer your quilt. Some battings may need to be prewashed, while others should definitely *not* be prewashed; be sure to check the manufacturer's instructions.

Layering the Quilt

Once your quilt top has been marked, your backing pieced and pressed, and your batting has "relaxed," you are ready to layer the quilt. Spread the backing wrong side up on a flat, clean surface; anchor it with pins or masking tape. Spread the batting over the backing, smoothing out any

wrinkles; then, center the quilt top on the backing, face up. Be careful not to stretch or distort any of the layers as you work. Starting in the middle, pin-baste the three layers together, gently smoothing any fullness to the sides and corners.

Now, baste the three layers together with a long needle and light-colored thread; start in the center and work diagonally to each corner, making a large X. Continue basting, laying in a grid of horizontal and vertical lines 6"–8" apart. Finish by running a line of stitches around the outside edges of the quilt.

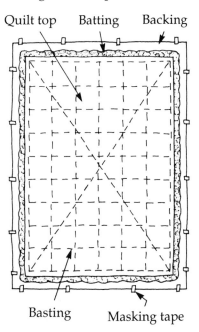

Quilt top Batting Backing

Basting Masking tape

Quilting and Tying Techniques

The purpose of quilting or tying is to keep the three layers together and to prevent the batting from lumping or shifting. Typically, quilts are tied (with knots either on the front or the back), tacked, or machine- or hand-quilted.

Machine Quilting

Machine quilting is suitable for all types of quilts, from baby and bed quilts that will be washed frequently to glamorous pieces for the wall. With machine quilting, you can quickly complete quilts that might otherwise languish on shelves. Unless you plan to stitch "in the ditch," mark the quilting lines *before* you layer the quilt. Consider using a simple allover grid or a continuous-line quilting design. Basting for machine quilting is often done with safety pins; if you have a large work surface to support the quilt and an even-feed foot for your sewing machine, you should have no problem with shifting layers or untidy pleats, tucks, and bubbles on the back side. Remove the safety pins as you sew. Pull thread ends to the back and work them into the quilt for a professional look.

Traditional Hand Quilting

To quilt by hand, you will need short, sturdy needles (called "Betweens"), quilting thread, and a thimble to fit the middle finger of your sewing hand. Most quilters also use a frame or hoop to support their work. Quilting needles run from size 3 to 12; the bigger the number, the smaller the needle. Use the smallest needle you can comfortably handle; the smaller the needle, the smaller your stitches will be.

Thread your needle with a single strand of quilting thread about 18" long; make a small knot and insert the needle in the top layer about 1" from the place where you want to start stitching. Pull the needle out at the point where quilting will begin and gently pull the thread until the knot pops through the fabric and into the batting. Begin your quilting line with a backstitch, inserting the needle straight down *through all three layers*. Proceed by taking small, even running stitches, rocking the needle up and down through all the layers until you have three or four stitches on the needle. Place your other hand underneath the quilt so you can feel the needle point with the tip of your finger when a stitch is taken.

To end a line of quilting, make a small knot close to the last stitch; then, backstitch, running the thread through the batting a needle's length. Gently pull the thread until the knot pops into the batting; clip the thread at the surface of the quilt. Remove basting stitches as you quilt, leaving only those that go around the outside edges of the quilt.

Starting and ending the quilting thread

Utility Quilting

Utility quilting is faster than traditional hand quilting, but "homier" than machine quilting; you use big needles and heavy threads (like perle cotton, several strands of embroidery floss, or Knit-Cro-Sheen™) and take nice big stitches, anywhere from ⅛" to ¼" in length. The method is well worth considering for casual, scrappy quilts and for pieces you might otherwise plan to machine quilt.

You can do utility quilting "freehand," without marking the quilt top, or mark quilting lines as usual. Use the shortest, thinnest, sharp-pointed needle you can get the thread through; try several different kinds to find the needle that works best for you. I like working with #8 perle cotton and a #6 Between needle. Keep your stitches as straight and even as possible.

Crow Footing and Other Tacking Techniques

Crow footing is done with a long needle and thick thread, such as a single or double strand of perle cotton or Knit-Cro-Sheen™. Isolated fly stitches are worked in a grid across the surface of the quilt; there are no visible knots or dangling threads.

Put your work in a hoop or frame. Use a long, sharp-pointed needle—cotton darners, millinery needles, or soft-sculpture needles. Make a small knot in the thread and insert the needle in the top layer of the quilt about 1" from A as shown in the diagram on page 35. Pull the needle out at A and gently pull the thread until the knot pops through the fabric and into the batting. Hold the thread down with the thumb and insert the needle at B, as shown; *go through all three layers* and bring the needle out at C. Insert the needle at D and travel *through the top layer only* to start the next stitch at A. This leaves a small diagonal stitch on the back of the quilt. Work in rows from the top to the bottom or from the right to the left of the quilt, spacing the stitches about 2" apart. To end stitching, bring the needle out at C and make a small knot about ⅛" from the surface of the quilt. Make a backstitch at D, running the thread through the batting an inch or so; pop the knot into the batting and clip the thread at the surface of the quilt.

1. Go through all three layers

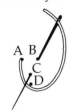

3. Work in rows, spacing the stitches about 2" apart

2. Travel through the top layer only

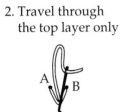

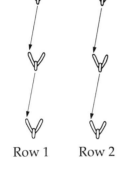

Row 1   Row 2

Backstitch tacking is another option. There are two different approaches—the Mennonite Tack and the Methodist Knot. Both stitches are best worked from the right to the left rather than from the top to the bottom of the quilt; they leave a small horizontal stitch on the back of the quilt.

To do the Mennonite Tack, bring the needle out at A as shown in the diagram below and take a backstitch about ¼" long *through all three layers*, coming back up just a few threads from the starting point (B–C). Reinsert the needle at D and travel *through the top layer only* to start the next stitch. The tiny second stitch, which should be almost invisible, crosses over the backstitch and locks the tacking.

1. Go through all three layers.

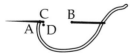

2. Travel through the top layer only.

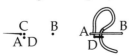

3. Work in rows from right to left.

The Methodist Knot is done with two backstitches. Bring the needle out at A as shown in the diagram below and take a backstitch *through all three layers*, coming back up beyond the starting point (B–C). Reinsert the needle at A and travel *through the top layer only* to start the next stitch.

1. Go through all three layers.

2. Travel through the top layer only to start the next stitch.

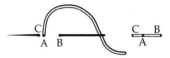

Any of these tacking stitches can be laid in at random, rather than on a uniform grid. Early quiltmakers who used these techniques often worked with the quilt stretched on a large floor frame, rolling in the edges of the quilt as the rows of tacking were completed, eliminating the need for basting. Small quilts can be tied or tacked without basting if the layers are spread smoothly over a table or other large, flat work surface.

Bindings

When the tying or quilting is complete, prepare for binding by removing any remaining basting threads, except for the stitches around the outside edge of the quilt. Trim the batting and backing even with the edge of the quilt top. Use a rotary cutter and ruler to get accurate, straight edges; make sure the corners are square.

Make enough binding to go around the perimeter of the quilt, plus about 18". The general instructions below are based on ⅜" (finished) double-fold binding, made from strips cut 2½" wide and stitched to the outside edges of the quilt with a ⅜" seam. Cutting dimensions for bindings in other sizes are given at the end of this section.

Straight-grain binding is fine for most applications. Simply cut strips from the lengthwise or crosswise grain of the fabric;

one crosswise strip will yield about 40" of binding. For ⅜" (finished) binding, cut the strips 2½" wide. Trim the ends of the strips at a 45° angle and seam the ends to make a continuous long strip; press seams open. Fold the strip in half lengthwise, wrong sides together, and press.

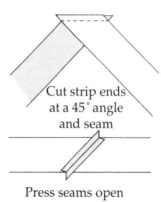

Press seams open

Use bias binding if your quilt edge contains curves or if you expect the quilt to get heavy use; binding cut on the bias does wear longer.

For a binding with mitered corners, start near the center of one side of the quilt. Lay the binding on the front of the quilt, lining up the raw edges of the binding with the raw edges of the quilt. Using an even-feed foot, sew the binding to the quilt with a seam the same size as the finished width of the binding—for ⅜" (finished) binding, use a ⅜" seam. Leave the first few inches of the binding loose so that you can join or overlap the beginning and ending of the binding strip later. Be careful not to stretch the quilt or the binding as you sew. When you reach the corner, stop the stitching a seam's width from the edge of the quilt and backstitch; clip threads.

Turn the quilt to prepare for sewing along the next edge. Fold the binding up and away from the quilt; then, fold it again to bring it even with the edge of the quilt. There will be an angled fold at the corner; the straight fold should be even with the top edge of the quilt.

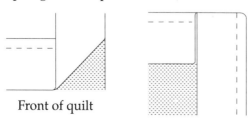

Front of quilt

Stitch from the straight fold in the binding to the next corner, pinning as necessary to keep the binding lined up with the raw edge of the quilt. When you reach the next corner, stop the stitching a seam's width from the edge of the quilt and backstitch; clip threads. Fold the binding as you did at the previous corner and continue around the edge of the quilt. When you reach the starting point, fold one end of the binding at a 45° angle; overlap the fold with the other end of the binding and finish stitching.

Fold the binding to the back, over the raw edges of the quilt; the folded edge of the binding should just cover the machine stitching line. Blindstitch the binding in place, making sure your stitches do not go through to the front of the quilt. At the corners, fold the binding to form miters on the front and back of the quilt; stitch the folds in the miters in place.

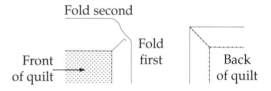

Strip widths for double-fold bindings in various finished sizes are cut as follows:

¼" binding	1¾"-wide strips
⅜" binding	2½"-wide strips
½" binding	3¼"-wide strips
⅝" binding	4"-wide strips
¾" binding	4¾"-wide strips

Labels

Be sure to sign and date your work! At the very least, embroider your name and the year the quilt was completed on the front or back of the quilt. Quilt historians and the future owners of your quilts will be interested in knowing more than just the "who" and "when"—consider tacking a handwritten or typed label to the back of the quilt that includes the name of the quilt, your name, your city and state, the date, for whom the quilt was made and why, and any other interesting or important information about the quilt.

Iron the label fabric to a piece of plastic-coated freezer paper to stabilize it while you write or type. For a handwritten label, use a permanent marking pen; a multi-strike ribbon should be used for typewritten labels. Always test to be absolutely sure the ink is permanent! Hand- or typewritten labels that safely pass the washing-machine test sometimes run and bleed when they are dry-cleaned.

Fold

Appliquéd handle for Basket block, p. 10
Add seam allowances

Stem
Add seam allowances

Appliquéd stem for Maple Leaf block, p. 20

Tree trunk

Trunk for Temperance Tree block, p. 28

PLANNING YOUR OWN SCRAPSAVER QUILT

Perhaps you'd like to arrange your ScrapSaver blocks in a setting different from the one shown. Many quilters like to make scrap blocks with no particular quilt in mind; they plan their quilts after they have completed a number of blocks.

Planning usually begins with a decision about quilt size. If you are making a quilt for the wall, the design and proportion of the piece is often more important than the size. Quilts for beds, on the other hand, must fit the beds for which they are intended. For bed quilts, I usually work within general parameters that give me a little room for design flexibility.

	Width	Length
Baby	36" to 45"	45" to 54"
Crib	42" to 48"	54" to 60"
Nap	54" to 60"	68" to 76"
Twin	56" to 64"	84" to 100"
Double	70" to 80"	84" to 100"
Queen	76" to 84"	90" to 104"
King	92" to 100"	90" to 104"

While some quilts are planned so that the pattern or design extends to the outside edges, most quilts have a patterned center section surrounded by borders. Decisions you make about the number and layout of the individual blocks will determine the overall dimensions of the patterned section. Use the work sheets on these pages to lay out this section of your quilt. Calculate the size of the patterned section from your sketched layout; then, decide on a border width that will bring the quilt to the desired dimensions. Your paper quilt plan will make it easy to tell how many blocks and setting pieces you need to make the patterned section of the quilt.

1	2	3	4	5	6	7	8	9	10	11	12
2											
3											
4											
5											
6											
7											
8											
9											
10											
11											
12											
13											
14											
15											

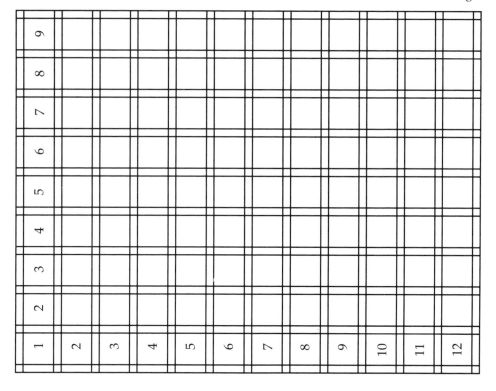

To find finished diagonal measurement of block,
multiply finished block size by 1.414.

That Patchwork Place Publications

The Americana Collection (Liberty Eagle, Old Glory, Stars and Stripes, and *Uncle Sam)*
by Nancy Southerland-Holmes
Angelsong by Joan Vibert
Angle Antics by Mary Hickey
Appliqué Borders: An Added Grace by Jeana Kimball
Baby Quilts from Grandma by Carolann M. Palmer
Back to Square One by Nancy J. Martin
Baltimore Bouquets by Mmi Dietrich
A Banner Year by Nancy J. Martin
Basket Garden by Mary Hickey
Blockbuster Quilts by Margaret J. Miller
Calendar Quilts by Joan Hanson
Cathedral Window: A Fresh Look by Nancy J. Martin
Copy Art for Quilters by Nancy J. Martin
Country Threads by Connie Tesene and Mary Tendall
Even More by Trudie Hughes
Fantasy Flowers: Pieced Flowers for Quilters by Doreen Cronkite Burbank
Feathered Star Sampler by Marsha McClaskey
Fit To Be Tied by Judy Hopkins
Five- and Seven-Patch Blocks & Quilts for the ScrapSaver™ by Judy Hopkins
Four-Patch Blocks & Quilts for the ScrapSaver™by Judy Hopkins
Handmade Quilts by Mimi Dietrich
Happy Endings—Finishing the Edges of Your Quilt by Mimi Dietrich
Holiday Happenings by Christal Carter
Home for Christmas by Nancy J. Martin and Sharon Stanley
In The Beginning by Sharon Evans Yenter
Lessons in Machine Piecing by Marsha McCloskey
Little By Little: Quilts in Miniature by Mary Hickey
More Template-Free™ *Quiltmaking* by Trudie Hughes
My Mother's Quilts: Designs from the Thirties by Sara Nephew
Nifty Ninepatches by Carolann M. Palmer
Not Just Quilts by Jo Parrott
Ocean Waves by Marsha McCloskey and Nancy J. Martin
One-of-a-Kind Quilts by Judy Hopkins
Pineapple Passion by Nancy Smith and Lynda Milligan
A Pioneer Doll and Her Quilts by Mary Hickey
Pioneer Storybook Quilts by Mary Hickey
Quilts to Share by Janet Kime
Red and Green: An Appliqué Tradition by Jeana Kimball
Reflections of Baltimore by Jeana Kimball
Rotary Riot: 40 Fast and Fabulous Quilts by Judy Hopkins and Nancy J. Martin
Scrap Happy by Sally Schneider
Shortcuts: A Concise Guide to Metric Rotary Cutting by Donna Lynn Thomas
Shortcuts: A Concise Guide to Rotary Cutting by Donna Lynn Thomas
Small Talk by Donna Lynn Thomas
Stars and Stepping Stones by Marsha McCloskey
Tea Party Time: Romantic Quilts and Tasty Tidbits by Nancy J. Martin
Template-Free™ *Quiltmaking* by Trudie Hughes
Template-Free™ *Quilts and Borders* by Trudie Hughes
Threads of Time by Nancy J. Martin
Women and Their Quilts by Nancyann Johanson Twelker

Tools

6" Bias Square®	8" Bias Square®
Metric Bias Square®	BiRangle™
Pineapple Rule	Rotary Mate™
Rotary Rule™	ScrapSaver™

Video
Shortcuts to America's Best-Loved Quilts

Many titles are available at your local quilt shop. For more information, send $2 for a color catalog to That Patchwork Place, Inc., PO Box 118, Bothell WA 98041-0118.